CW01677625

# Close Encounters

**Family Lenten meditations on those whose lives were touched by Jesus**

Eleanor Watkins

kevin mayhew

First published in 2006 by

KEVIN MAYHEW LTD
Buxhall, Stowmarket, Suffolk, IP14 3BW
E-mail: info@kevinmayhewltd.com
Web: www.kevinmayhew.com



9 8 7 6 5 4 3 2 1 0

ISBN 184417 705 X
Catalogue No 1500962

Cover design by Chris Coe
Typesetting by Richard Weaver

Printed in Great Britain

# Contents

# Introduction

When preparing to write this series of studies for Lent, I read again the Gospel accounts of the life of Jesus. As I read, I was struck by the ways in which he interacted with the people he met. Jesus was definitely a 'people person'. From his early days, he loved people – loved to mix, to talk, to eat and relax with them, to have fun at social events, to share the happenings of their lives. When his ministry began in earnest, Jesus dealt in love and compassion with the needs of those who came to him. No one was too humble or insignificant to be noticed by him. He was never too busy or too occupied to pause to speak to someone who specially needed him. No one called out to him in vain. Most of those who met him went home joyfully praising God because of their encounter with the Saviour. He was comfortable at all levels of society, from wealthy leaders to the poorest beggar. He accepted invitations to all kinds of homes, and even sometimes invited himself. He was a man who truly loved people.

Not one person who met Jesus remained unchanged or untouched by the encounter. Not all received him and his teaching; there were those who chose to reject him, and who afterwards had bitter regrets. But those who did receive him were rewarded by immeasurable joy, love, peace and hope, as well as work to do in his kingdom.

These are the stories of some of the people who met Jesus during his 33 short years on the earth. May you meet with Jesus himself as you read, and be blessed by a fresh encounter with him this Eastertide.

*Eleanor Watkins*

# Mary
## Blessed among women

Day 1

The angel said: *'Greetings, Mary!'*

She said: *'Why have you come? I am afraid.'*

The angel said: *'Don't be afraid. You have found favour with God.'*

She said: *'I am just a young girl.'*

The angel said: *'You will have a son. He will be a mighty king and he will be called Jesus.'*

She said: *'How can this be? I'm not even married. I am a virgin.'*

The angel said: *'This will be God's son. Nothing is impossible to those who obey him.'*

She said: *'May the will of God be done.'*

Eleanor Watkins, *Going with God*, Kevin Mayhew 1999

**Reading:** Luke 1:26-38

We owe a great deal to Mary of Nazareth. A young girl, barely old enough to be married, living in a male-dominated society in an occupied land; yet God chose her to be the mother of the one who would bring redemption to a sin-sick world.

Mary was greatly troubled, both by the appearance of the angel and by the message he brought. If what he promised came true, the repercussions would be terrifying. Her pregnancy would bring shame to herself and her family, to Joseph, and to their community. Tongues would wag, fingers would be pointed and her reputation would be in tatters.

Yet Mary chose to believe God. She had an obedient childlike heart and put herself into the hands of her heavenly Father, understanding very little of what was to come. She trusted God and gave her consent to his plan.

What would have happened if she had been too frightened, too apprehensive, too overwhelmed to agree? Would God have raised up someone else to be the mother of his Son, or devised a plan B?

Maybe. But Mary said yes to God. She walked a step at a time in obedience to her Father, brought her child into the world, nurtured and loved him with a mother's joy as he grew to boyhood and then manhood, and saw her task through to the end.

**Reflection:** *Do we need to see a 'blueprint' before we can agree to God's purposes for our lives? Can we walk with him, a step at a time, trusting him to provide all we need to take the next step? Can we trust him enough to accept that there will be sorrow and hardship as well as joy in his plans for us, but that ultimately it will be 'turned into glory'?*

**Prayer:** *Lord, draw me so close that, like Mary, I will obey without question, knowing that all your ways are perfect.*

# Elizabeth
## Fitting into God's timetable

Day 2

*Now is the accepted time; behold, now is the day of salvation.*
2 Corinthians 6:2 King James

**Reading:** Luke 1:39-56

Jewish women wanted children, and in particular, sons. Such was the status of a woman with a son, that the boy's name would be inscribed upon her hands. Children were a gift of God and a sign of his favour; there was disgrace and diminishment in being childless.

Zechariah and Elizabeth must have prayed and longed for children for most of their married life. Both were now into old age, with Elizabeth long past the age for childbearing. Even when Zechariah was told by Gabriel himself that they would have a child, he had doubts and questions. Maybe the news of a son who would be 'a joy and delight, whose birth would bring rejoicing to many' was just too good to be believed.

However, it happened, and Elizabeth rejoiced in her pregnancy. In her sixth month, she was visited by her cousin Mary from Nazareth in Galilee, newly pregnant herself, unmarried, and seeking breathing space to come to terms with her situation before the news leaked out and the wrath of the righteous came down on her head. The moment Elizabeth heard Mary's voice, the Holy Spirit fell upon her in power, and her unborn baby 'leaped for joy'. Both Elizabeth and her unborn son immediately recognised that the baby Mary carried would be their own Saviour and Lord. What comfort and affirmation for Mary, as both expectant mothers praised the Lord with hearts filled with joy!

Mary's visit with Elizabeth lasted for three months. This must have been a precious time for them both, a time of strengthening and encouraging as they looked forward to the births. Mary probably fetched and carried for Elizabeth as her pregnancy advanced, while Mary learned much wisdom from her cousin's long life experience. Maybe they sewed small garments and speculated delightfully about the sons they would have. As yet, no warning shadow had fallen over the lives of their boys.

Zechariah and Elizabeth's prayers could have been answered years earlier. By this time, they could have been grandparents or even great-grandparents. But God was preparing them for a special task. They had lived upright and blameless lives, and their years of righteous living experience would prepare them for the task of training and moulding this boy in his earliest years. He would have a sound foundation for the task before him. This was the time God had chosen for Elizabeth's child.

**Reflection:** *What is our reaction when our prayers are not answered as and when we would like? Do we give up? Persevere? Go on praying even when hope seems gone? Think of examples from your own life when God's timing in answering prayer has proved to be the greater blessing.*

**Prayer:** *The Lord hath given me my petition which I asked of him. (1 Samuel 1:27 King James)*

# Joseph

## Faithful father

Day 3

> *And the child grew and became strong; he was filled with wisdom, and the grace of God was upon him.* Luke 2:40 NIV
>
> *And Jesus grew in wisdom and stature, and in favour with God and men.* Luke 2:52 NIV

Joseph the carpenter was clearly a man of character, being regarded by the Lord as righteous (*Matthew 1:19*). He also proved to be a man of compassion. A girl in his fiancée Mary's condition, found to be pregnant out of wedlock, could be subject to the harshest judgements, even stoning. Joseph must have been bitterly hurt and disappointed to be told of her pregnancy, knowing the baby was not his. But, for her sake, he was prepared to quietly dissolve the marriage agreement and let her go without punishment.

After being told in a dream of the nature of Mary's child, Joseph gladly and willingly took on the role of parenting and nurturing the child Jesus. His home must have been a lively, bustling, busy place, with at least six younger children, maybe more. It was not a wealthy household, nor a poor one, just an ordinary home. Everyone would have had their tasks to do. There would have been love and laughter as well as careful training. And it worked. Joseph's faithful and loving parenting paid off.

Many children are raised by people not their parents by blood. In our modern society, the 'nuclear' family of mum, dad and kids is no longer the norm. There are single parents (dads as well as mums) step brothers and sisters, endless combinations of half-siblings, children raised by grandparents, aunts and uncles, foster or adoptive parents. I have been blessed with four children, and, to date, four grandchildren. Out of those eight people, only three are related to me by blood. But all our bonds are every bit as strong as blood ties.

Not all children being raised by people not their 'real' parents live in dysfunctional families. There are many wonderful step, adoptive and other parents who are bringing up balanced, secure and loved young people. Maybe they need a greater degree of commitment, caring, wisdom and perspective than 'ordinary' families. A sense of humour is vital! And it helps enormously to have support from the wider family, friends, and a strong church fellowship.

**Reflection:** *Think about people you know who have step-children, adopted or foster kids. Is there anything you can do to help and support them, especially those who are finding the going difficult? Could you provide a safe (and non-judgemental) haven for a struggling parent to come to, to talk, relax, chill out, and (hopefully) find refreshment? Can we pray that kids will 'grow in wisdom and stature' – and keep praying when problems arise?*

**Prayer:** *Dear Father of us all, help us in our parenting and in all our dealings with the young. If we are older, help us to guide and encourage younger families to bring up godly children. And thank you that, to all of us of whatever age, you remain a loving and faithful Father. Amen.*

# Herod
## Under threat

Day 4

*A voice is heard in Ramah, weeping and great mourning, Rachel weeping for her children and refusing to be comforted, because they are no more.* Matthew 2:18 NIV

King Herod was scared. As ruler of Judea, he valued his position and hung on to it with all his might. The news of a new and greater king had him badly rattled. This must be stopped in its tracks. Failing to trick the Magi into revealing the exact whereabouts of the baby king, he took drastic measures. All the little boys under two years old in Bethlehem and its vicinity would have to go. The Slaughter of the Innocents goes down in history as the unspeakably barbaric act of a cruel tyrant under threat.

Sadly, the slaughtering of innocents has gone on down through the ages and goes on still. Children die the painful and horrible deaths of war victims in conflicts for which they bear no responsibility. Children suffer and die from starvation, AIDS and other treatable conditions in third world countries; they die of neglect and abuse in every country in the world; they die in squalor on the streets and in sewers; they die in the pristine sterile surroundings of abortion clinics, or gasp out their last breaths in a bucket because their parents dared have one child above their quota.

God has stern warnings for those who fail to protect and care for the innocent and vulnerable. Jesus said it was better for the perpetrators to be drowned attached to a heavy weight than to harm one of these little ones. All of us bear responsibility for the young, whether or not we are parents ourselves. Let us look that responsibility squarely in the face.

**Reflection:** *Are there distressing issues that we find it easier to turn a blind eye to: i.e. the use of child labour, the practice of child prostitution – even the subtle erosion of parents' rights that seems to be happening*

*right here in our own nation? How can we make our voices heard effectively to change things? Are there ways we could help needy children worldwide, through regular donations, child sponsorship or participating in aid projects? Can we offer practical help to families we know who may be struggling? Can we make it a priority to pray and intercede for children and young people everywhere?*

**Prayer:** *Lord, we thank you for all children everywhere. They are our treasure, our hope and our future. Help us to value, nurture, cherish and love them. Help us to fight injustice to children, to guard their innocence, to protect them from all evil and to let them know that they are precious in your sight. Amen.*

# John the Baptist
## A shining light

Day 5

*You are the light of the world. A city on a hill cannot be hidden. Neither do people light a lamp and put it under a bowl. Instead they put it on its stand, and it gives light to everyone in the house. In the same way, let your light shine before men, that they may see your good deeds and praise your Father in heaven.* Matthew 5:14-16 NIV

The Gospel accounts seem to indicate that John was an austere, intense, rather fierce kind of man. Living rough in the desert regions around the Jordan, wearing clothes of coarse camel hair and leather, and eating locusts and wild honey, he was definitely different! He was certainly not afraid to speak his mind, either, addressing the Pharisees and Sadducees as a 'generation of vipers' and calling on people to repent of their sins and turn from their sinful lifestyles. Yet the people flocked to the desert to listen to him, to repent, and to be baptised by him. Their hearts were hungry.

Some wondered whether John could be the promised Messiah, but he was quick to put them right, declaring himself only a fore-runner and preparer of the way for the one who would be the true Light of the World.

In a scene from the 1977 film *Close Encounters of the Third Kind,* the main characters have travelled through many difficulties to reach the mountain base where the big spaceship is to come in. As they wait expectantly and the excitement grows, a number of small spacecraft streak and soar through the night sky, lights twinkling and sparkling, some small, some larger, while every-one watches and eagerly wonders if each is the expected one. At last, when the big ship comes in, it is so huge, so dazzling, so magnificent and majestic that it seems to fill the sky, and no one can be in any doubt that this is the one.

John was not the 'light of the world', and he was quick to describe himself as not even worthy to unloose the straps of the sandals Jesus wore, and reluctant at first to baptise him in water. He had come to prepare the way for his Lord, and was content to step back and let Jesus take his rightful place.

Yet Jesus described John, too, as a 'lamp lit and shining', who had his part to play in bringing light to a dark and sin-sick world. Later, he told his disciples that they, also, carried that light, and that they, and we, must keep our lamps lit and shining brightly.

**Reflection:** *Think of the ways in which Christians can be described as lights of the world. Imagine how it would be if there were no Christians in today's society. Are there those in your own local community who shine brightly? How can we keep our own lamps clear and bright?*

**Prayer:** *Let our light so shine before men, that they may see our good works and glorify our Father in heaven.*

# Andrew
## The first disciple

Day
6

> *Andrew, Simon Peter's brother, was one of the two who heard what John had said and who had followed Jesus. The first thing Andrew did was to find his brother Simon and tell him, 'We have found the Messiah!' Then he brought Simon to Jesus.* John 1:40-42 NIV

There is not a great deal of reference to the disciple Andrew in the Gospels. We know that he was one of the first men to leave his everyday work as a fisherman and follow Jesus. Andrew seems to have been gifted at linking others with the Lord. It was he who brought forward the boy with the loaves and fishes to feed over five thousand hungry people *(John 6:8-9)*. Later, with Philip, he approached Jesus with a request from some Greeks who wanted to see him *(John 12:20-22)*. But most notably, as soon as he had heard the message Jesus brought, Andrew went in search of his brother so that he, too, could hear the good news.

In days to come, it was Andrew's brother Simon Peter who would spring into prominence as one of the stalwarts of the Christian faith. Andrew himself largely fades into the background, though legend has it that he was crucified for his faith on a Cross Soltaire – an X-shaped cross that is represented in white on a blue ground on the Scottish flag.

The relationship of brothers is an important one in Middle Eastern cultures. In Muslim communities especially, it is common to see brothers walking hand in hand with fingers interlaced. A man is expected to look out for his brother and take responsibility for him. Andrew was overjoyed when he found the Messiah and couldn't wait for his brother to find him too.

Bearing witness to our faith in Christ is not always an easy thing to do, and perhaps most difficult of all within our own families. Someone I know called Amy, bubbling over with joy at her new-found life in Jesus, couldn't wait to share it with her family. Her young brother's crushing reply was, 'Well, you might think you're different, but *I* know you're the same horrid little brat you always were!' She said she really had no reply to that. But Amy's life since, which has seen more tragic and crushing loss than almost anyone I know, has clearly proved the strength of the rock her feet stand upon. Maybe it's our changed lives, rather than what we say, that count most in the eyes of those close to us.

**Reflection:** *St Francis of Assisi said, 'Preach the Gospel always. When necessary, use words.' It's been said that if we want to know the Christian status of someone, ask the people they live with. How does this make us feel about the way we live within our own families? Do we always show our nearest and dearest the same patience, forgiveness, kindness and courtesy that we show to others?*

*How can we best share Jesus with our family members?*

**Prayer:** *Teach us to see Jesus in the members of our families, especially in their distressing disguises.*

As adapted from Mother Teresa's *Prayer for Families*

## Levi

### Ready to follow

Day 7

*After this, Jesus went out and saw a tax collector by the name of Levi sitting at his tax booth. 'Follow me,' Jesus said to him, and Levi got up, left everything and followed him. Then Levi held a great banquet for Jesus at his house, and a large crowd of tax collectors and others were eating with them. But the Pharisees and the teachers of the law who belonged to their sect complained to his disciples, 'Why do you eat and drink with tax collectors and "sinners"?' Jesus answered them, 'It is not the healthy who need a doctor, but the sick. I have not come to call the righteous, but sinners to repentance.'*

Luke 5:27-32 NIV

Taxation employees are maybe not the most popular members of any society. Recently we were visited by a tax official who had come to reassess my husband's business premises, and I admit with shame that it took a certain amount of teeth-gritting for me to be willing to offer him a cup of tea!

But in the days of Jesus, tax collectors were numbered among the vilest of the vile. Working for their Roman masters to gather the enforced taxes from their Jewish contemporaries, they were often dishonest and corrupt, feathering their own nests at the expense of their countrymen. They were looked on as thieves, extortionists and, worst of all, traitors to their nation.

Levi (also called Matthew, who would be the author of one of the Gospels) was obviously a wealthy man. He would have had a comfortable lifestyle in the pay of the Roman occupiers. He had a lot to lose. By then, huge crowds were beginning to follow Jesus, and Levi would almost certainly have heard something of his teaching. The moment Jesus noticed him at his tax booth and said simply, 'Follow me!', Levi did just that. His heart was ready, and he had recognised the truth when it came.

Jesus was the honoured guest at Levi's dinner party soon afterwards. Levi had asked all his tax-collector friends along, wanting them to find the new life in Jesus for themselves. The Pharisees were full of righteous indignation, immediately trying to put a wedge between Jesus and his disciples by calling into question their socialising with 'sinners'.

The reply of Jesus summed up his purpose in a nutshell. It was not the 'righteous' he had come to save, for they felt no need of a Saviour. It was the sinner, the one who acknowledged his need and came with a humble heart to receive that salvation.

**Reflection:** *It is all too easy to judge people, as Levi was judged, by outward appearance and lifestyle, not seeing what goes on in the heart. Think of examples where we make snap judgements: wealthy people must be arrogant, those on benefit are surely work-shy, a teenager in a hoodie must be up to no good, for example.*

*Are we willing to take time to get to know the real person, despite appearances?*

**Prayer:** *Lord, help me, in my limited way, to see others as you see them. Give me a heart that is prepared to reach out. Help me not to fear or distrust those who are 'different', those I might not be quite comfortable around. And let your love flow through me to them.*

# The Leper
## Touched by compassion

Day 8

*While Jesus was in one of the towns, a man came along who was covered with leprosy. When he saw Jesus, he fell with his face to the ground and begged him, 'Lord, if you are willing, you can make me clean.' Jesus reached out his hand and touched the man. 'I am willing,' he said. 'Be clean.' And immediately the leprosy left him.*

Luke 5:12-13 NIV

Leprosy was a fearful disease. There was no prospect of a cure, it was horribly disfiguring and crippling, and thought to be highly infectious; it isolated sufferers from their families and their communities; it carried a shame and a stigma. Anyone touching a leper became unclean, and had to be ceremonially cleansed themselves.

The leper was desperate. Strictly speaking, he should have stayed outside the town limits away from where people were. But having nothing to lose, he defied the rules and grabbed at this last chance of help from the one who was going about healing the sick. And he showed a surprising awareness of the nature of that person. 'Lord, if you are willing, you can make me clean.'

The response of Jesus was immediate. 'I am willing! Be clean!' And he reached out to touch the man.

This healing did not exactly advance the ministry of Jesus. When told to say nothing, but to present himself to the priest for the ritual cleansing required before rejoining society, the man disobeyed. Maybe he was so carried away he could not contain his excitement. Anyway, he told everyone he met, and the result was that the crowds came in such numbers that Jesus could not carry out his purposes of teaching and preaching. But he had acted true to his nature. He had responded to the faith in the mercy of God that the leper had shown.

In our present day, healing ministries are sometimes used as attractions to draw in crowds so that they will hear the gospel message. Jesus needed no such gimmicks. The crowds flocked wherever he was healing and teaching, often bringing his ministry to a standstill. Yet in spite of that, he still made time for that one sick man, he still responded with immediate compassion, he still reached out and touched the untouchable.

**Reflection:** *Are we sometimes tempted to disregard the demands of the individual, who might take our time or distract us from our own 'important' ministries? Are there those in our communities who are regarded as 'untouchable' – HIV or AIDS victims, the mentally sick or disadvantaged, addicts, immigrants, the homeless? How many times have we hurried past huddled figures on the streets or in shop doorways on the way to urgent appointments? I know I have done this.*

*What can we do in response to the heart cries of the desperate?*

**Prayer:** *Soften my heart, Lord, soften my heart,*
*from all indifference, set me apart,*
*to feel your compassion, to weep with your tears –*
*come soften my heart, O Lord, soften my heart.*

Graham Kendrick, © *1988 Make Way Music*

# The Paralysed Man
## The faith of friends

Day 9

*Now to him who is able to do immeasurably more than all we ask or imagine, according to his power that is at work within us, to him be glory in the church and in Christ Jesus throughout all generations, for ever and ever! Amen.* Ephesians 3:20-21 NIV

**Reading:** Luke 5:17-26

We don't know whether the paralysed man had asked to be taken to Jesus, or whether it was totally the idea of his friends. In any event, they went to a great deal of trouble to get him to the house where Jesus was teaching. And there were no wheelchairs or lifts in those days! Carrying a helpless man on a mat over any distance is hard work, even for four people. And when they failed to push a pathway through the crowds around the doorway, they had no hesitation in hauling him to the rooftop and breaking a hole large enough to lower him through. I'm sure they were prepared to pay for roof repairs too!

Two things stand out:

1. They were true friends who were determined to get help for the disabled one.
2. They had faith in Jesus to heal.

In the event, they got more and better than they had asked for. The first act of Jesus, when the man appeared from above and landed before him, was to forgive the paralysed man his sins. Only after the other teachers began to murmur at his presumption did he also release the paralysis and enable the man to walk. We don't know the state of the man's faith, we're not even told if he'd repented of his sin, but we do know that after his encounter with Jesus he went home walking and praising God with all his might.

The faith and determination of the four friends had paid off.

Most of us have prayed for years for some of our friends and family members, and often nothing much seems to happen. The four friends could have given up when they saw the crowds, taken the man back home or left him somewhere that Jesus would hopefully pass by and notice him. But they persisted. God commends persistence *(Luke 18:1-8, 1 Thessalonians 5:17, James 5:16).*

As we bring those we care about into his presence, over and over again, in prayer, he will hear and answer. There may be practical things we need to do too, sometimes involving hard work and inconvenience. God will bless, maybe over and above anything we could expect.

**Reflection:** *Encounters with Jesus may not always follow the pattern we expect them to. God sometimes answers prayers in surprising ways. Think of some examples in your own experience. And thank God for those who prayed for you.*

**Prayer:** *Father, I bring to you those who don't seem able, or willing, to come to you themselves. Touch them in such a way that their lives are transformed and their hearts filled to overflowing with your praise.*

# Nicodemus
## Born twice

Day 10

*I tell you the truth, no one can see the kingdom of God unless he is born again.*
John 3:3 NIV

Read the whole of John chapter 3.

Nicodemus came to Jesus under cover of nightfall. A prominent person and respected teacher himself, he was careful of his reputation. Nevertheless, there were pressing questions in his heart and mind that demanded answers. Despite his learned status, he was still not sure about his own eternal destination.

When Jesus gave the simple answer, 'You must be born again,' Nicodemus hadn't a clue what he meant. This just couldn't happen in the ordinary way. And Jesus had to explain, in simple terms, with illustrations from the natural world, the workings of the Spirit in the heart of a man.

Maybe it all seemed too simple for Nicodemus. We've all met people who feel that there must be more to it than simply accepting from God the free gift of eternal life through Jesus Christ. Anyway, we are not told how he responded right then. Later, Nicodemus gives a word in defence of Jesus when he is under threat from the Pharisees and teachers (*John 7:50-51).* Later still, no longer concerned with his standing in the community, he takes the broken body of Jesus and lovingly and sacrificially prepares it for burial. It would seem that the words spoken by Jesus that night had taken root and blossomed in his heart and he had been 'born again' of the Spirit of God.

**Reflection:** *The term 'born again Christian' has come to be something of a sneering way of describing believers who appear to be 'over the top' and fanatical, as well as out of touch with the realities of our life and* *times. Yet it describes so accurately the beginning of a new life of faith, a putting away of the old, a fresh start.*

*To anyone in doubt about his or her eternal destiny, the answer is still the same: 'You must be born again.'*

**Prayer:** *Lord Jesus, thank you that you came into the world because you loved us. Thank you that you died in our place, that our sins might be forgiven and that we can have new life in you.*

*I come to you in repentance to receive that forgiveness and to accept from you that gift of eternal life. Thank you for your love and mercy. Amen.*

# The Centurion with a Sick Servant

## A man under authority

Day 11

*Freely you have received, freely give.* Matthew 10:8 NIV

**Reading:** Luke 7:1-10

The centurion was an important man, and he seems to have been a caring one too, well respected among the Jews. He had dispatched some Jewish elders to ask for the healing of his sick servant, and they pleaded his case earnestly, citing the help he had been to the Jewish nation, and saying that he 'deserved' the help of Jesus.

However, the centurion himself had other ideas. Before Jesus reached his house, he sent friends with the message that he felt quite unworthy to have Jesus come under his roof. He put forward no plea of 'deserving' a favour, but acknowledged that he, knowing the discipline of being under authority and obeying orders as well as giving them, recognised the authority of God's Son. He knew that Jesus only had to speak the word and the man would be healed. He trusted wholly in the mercy, power and authority of Jesus.

Jesus 'marvelled' at the faith of the centurion, and used the incident as an illustration to demonstrate real faith to the people who followed him. This man had grasped what it was all about.

How often do we feel that God must answer our prayers, or those of others, because they are deserved? Do we ever feel that because we've served faithfully, or prayed long, or worked our socks off, or gone the extra mile, God must surely give us what we ask for? There seems to be something in us that feels we can only accept something if it's deserved, or if we can offer something back. Have you ever felt frustrated, trying to give a gift, when the other person insists on giving something in return?

**Reflection:** *Think about why we often feel we must reciprocate when given a gift. What is it that makes us feel that way? Could it be subtle pride, a desire not to be indebted? Do we sometimes give with a (maybe subconscious) feeling that we might get something in return?*

*Meditate on how little we deserve salvation and how freely it is given.*

**Prayer:** *Grant us, O Lord, the grace freely to receive from you, and the willingness freely to give.*

# The Widow's Son

## Jesus is passing

Day 12

*Reach out and touch the Saviour as he passes by,*
*you'll find he's not too busy to hear your heart's cry,*
*he's passing at this moment, your needs to supply,*
*reach out and touch Jesus as he goes by.*

Bill Harman, © *Gospel Publishing House*

**Reading:** Luke 7:11-17

As usual, a large crowd accompanied Jesus as he approached the town called Nain. Almost there, they encountered another large group, a funeral procession leaving the town for the place of burial. A widowed mother wept at the loss of her only son, and the heart of Jesus was touched. He commanded the dead young man to get up, and he 'sat up and began to talk'. Because Jesus passed that way, tragedy and sorrow was turned to rejoicing.

The ministry of Jesus was an itinerant one. He moved around from place to place, village to village, never staying long in one place. We read, over and over again, of the people he encountered as he passed by. Without exception, all were changed by the meeting. Whether the need was for forgiveness, healing, correction, encouragement – or even restoration to life – Jesus, in his love and power, was able to supply that need.

It is a challenging thought to realise that each one of us who belongs to Jesus carries that same love and power, by the Holy Spirit. Wherever we go, Jesus goes too. He is in our homes, our schools, our workplaces, the supermarket, the High Street, the doctor's waiting room. Wherever we happen to be, there he is too. This is what he said would happen, and this is how 'the works he did, and greater works' are done.

Do we make a difference to the people we meet as we pass by? Do we see the needs of others and 'have compassion'? It may only be a word of comfort to a bereaved neighbour, a visit to an elderly person in our street, an invitation for coffee to a lonely newcomer in our area. Sometimes we never know the outcome, but whenever we reach out to others in love, they're touched by Jesus too.

**Reflection:** *Think of how many people we have the opportunity to bless during the day, even if it's just a shop assistant, the next-door neighbour, family members or work colleagues. Think of those we're in touch with by letter, phone or email. Ask God for opportunities to minister the love of Jesus to them.*

**Prayer:** *Lord, fill me afresh with the love and power of your Holy Spirit, so that I can overflow to those I meet.*

# The Sick Woman

## Just a touch

Day 13

*She only touched the hem of his garment as to his side she stole,*
*amid the crowd that gathered around him, and straightway she was whole.*
*Oh, touch the hem of his garment, and thou, too, shall be free;*
*his saving power this very hour shall give new life to thee.*

G. F. Root, *Redemption Hymnal*

**Reading:** Mark 5:25-34

This poor woman had suffered for a long time. She had spent all the money she had on doctors' bills, and put up with the pain and humiliation of various treatments, all to no avail. In fact, she was getting worse.To add insult to injury, the constant bleeding made her ceremonially unclean and she was isolated from others. Anyone who touched her would be unclean also, any furniture she sat on would be considered unclean, she would not even be allowed to prepare or cook food.

Into this lonely, painful, debilitating half-existence came news of a teacher from Galilee who was healing the sick wherever he went. No wonder she ignored the rules and joined the crowds that streamed out to follow him, though in her humility she would not presume to speak to him or ask anything of him. If she could quietly just touch the hem of the robe he wore, it would be enough. So she pressed through the surging throng, among the bony knees, knuckles and elbows, to get close enough, and reached out a trembling hand.

Jesus knew immediately; 'Who touched me?' he asked.

His disciples replied that any, or many, of the crowd could have pushed or jostled him, but Jesus knew that this was different. He had felt God's power move through him in blessing. The woman came forward, trembling, and fell at his feet. Jesus spoke tenderly to her, healed her sick body and pronounced her sins forgiven.

What was it that made the touch of the woman different to that of the pressing crowd? What made the healing power of Jesus respond even before he knew it?

Was it not the faith of the sick woman – not faith in any magic power that might be contained in the clothes that Jesus wore – but faith that he was indeed the Son of God with power to heal. A simple, childlike faith, maybe a weak and fearful one, but determined enough to risk the revulsion and disgust of the crowd, clear enough to recognise where her only help lay, and strong enough to reach out for it.

**Reflection:** *Do we have to have perfect understanding and a strong, educated faith, free of all doubt, before we can ask anything of God? Read what Matthew has to say about faith in 17:20.*

**Prayer:** *Lord, I thank you that each one of us has been granted a measure of faith.*

*Help us to put that faith into action, and see what you will accomplish because of it.*

# Jairus' Daughter
## In God's time

Day 14

*My times are in your hands.* Psalm 31:15 NIV

**Reading:** Mark 5:21-24, 35-43

This little girl would be the apple of her father's eye, the darling of the household. Just on the brink of womanhood, and from a privileged family, her whole future lay ahead of her.

But she was dying.

Jairus himself hurried to find Jesus and bring him to his house. Jesus as usual was surrounded and followed by crowds, and was further hindered when the sick woman needed help on the way. Jesus was in no hurry. He had entered our time span when he became human, but understood well that his Father God's timing is not the same as ours. Even when the servant came hurrying to tell him not to bother after all because the little girl had died, there was no panic, no pressure. Just reassurance that all would be well (*Mark 5:36)*.

Are we ever tempted to try to squeeze God and his purposes into our time spans? How often are we exhorted to evangelise, witness, pray and work, because we are in the last days and time is short? Of course, all these activities are right and needful. But we must do them as God directs, not in a panicky, driven, pressured kind of way. I've known people who desperately prayed for their loved ones, imploring God to save them before they themselves left this life. Sadly, many never saw their prayers answered – but, again, God's timing is not ours. He is the Lord of time and sees the end from the beginning.

Jesus routed the grieving crowd around the little girl, took her by the hand and told her to get up. Then he asked that she be given something to eat. No fuss, no rush, no panic. There was time enough for all his purposes.

**Reflection:** *Think for a while of the nature of time. Try to imagine a life where time no longer exists. Does this boggle the mind? It does mine!*

**Prayer:** *With the Lord a day is like a thousand years, and a thousand years are like a day (2 Peter 3:8 NIV).*

*Lord, help me to live in that knowledge.*

# The Woman at the Well
## Breaking the barriers

Day 15

*Jesus answered, 'Everyone who drinks this water will be thirsty again, but whoever drinks the water I give him will never thirst. Indeed, the water I give him will become in him a spring of water welling up to eternal life.* John 4:13-14 NIV

**Reading:** John 4:1-42

Women in the days of Jesus were very much second-class citizens. They had little status outside the home, no part in community affairs, and were not taught in the synagogues. Their opinions were not considered. A man would not speak to a woman in public, not even to his own wife.

Add to this the fact that the woman at the well was a despised Samaritan (*John 4:9*) and someone of doubtful reputation (*John 4:17-18*) and her meeting with Jesus seems all the more remarkable. In beginning a conversation with her, Jesus broke all the long-held traditions of the Jews.

1. The barrier of race. The Samaritans had intermarried and were despised by the Jews. They were considered inferior in every way, a mongrel race, not to be mixed with. Sadly, these racist views still exist in parts of today's world.
2. The barriers of belief. Samaritans worshipped in Mount Gerizim, the Jews in Jerusalem. Jews considered Samaritans to be heretics, and would not even eat or drink with them. Jesus broke all taboos by asking for a drink of water from the woman's water jar.
3. The barriers of gender. No respectable Jew, least of all a rabbi, would speak to a woman in public.
4. The barriers of reputation. People with the woman's track record would be shunned by Jewish society.

Jesus broke all the barriers by speaking to the woman at the well and offering her the 'living water' of salvation. And it didn't end there. Because of her encounter with Jesus, the gospel word spread widely in her community and in her country.

**Reflection:** *Think of those in today's world imprisoned by barriers of race, faith, sex or reputation. If these barriers are attacked by force, it often only succeeds in strengthening them. The ill-treatment of prisoners results in outrage and revenge. The mocking of others' religions only leads to boiling resentment and hatred. Jesus built bridges by one-to-one encounters. How can we reach out to those trapped behind barriers?*

**Prayer:** *Help me, O Lord, to reach out in some way to those imprisoned behind barriers, offering them the living water of salvation and freedom.*

# The Boy with the Loaves and Fishes

## Giving gladly

Day 16

*Here is a boy with five small barley loaves and two small fish . . .*

John 6:9 NIV

**Reading:** Mark 6:31-44

Jesus and his disciples were all exhausted and drained from the speaking and teaching they had been engaged in. In addition, the news had just come in of the brutal death of John the Baptist. No wonder they needed a break and a rest. For this reason, Jesus suggests that they take a boat and sail round the coast to a quiet place near Bethsaida.

However, it doesn't quite turn out as planned. Somehow, the news has leaked and people have set off on foot around the shoreline, gathering others as they go, so that by the time the boat lands, there are vast crowds waiting for it.

Characteristically, Jesus doesn't demand his rest, space and privacy. Once again, he 'has compassion', preaches and teaches, and heals the sick ones *(Mark 6:34)*.

When night falls, everyone is hungry and the disciples request Jesus to send the people away to find food. So spontaneous has been the gathering that the people have made no provision for meals, and the crowd is huge – five thousand men, not counting the women and children.

Instead, he makes the startling reply, '*You* give them something to eat.'

They stare in amazement. 'We have nothing! And no money to buy food for them.'

'Go and see what you have,' he answers. No one comes up with much until Andrew brings forward a boy with five small loaves and two fish, probably a packed lunch provided by the boy's mother *(John 6:8-9)*. Anyway, he offers it willingly, Jesus blesses the food and begins to distribute it and miraculously, it stretches and stretches and stretches, feeding everyone with lots to spare.

In the hands of Jesus, a little, offered gladly, can become much. It's not the quantity that counts, but the willing heart behind it. A widow is commended for giving all she has *(Mark 12:42-43)*. A boy's picnic feeds thousands. We may not be able to give much, but what we can give – of money, time, talents, anything we have – can be multiplied a million times as we offer it to Jesus.

**Reflection:** *Sometimes we feel that the little we have to offer is hardly worth giving.*

*Or when we don't have much we're tempted to hang on to what we have. Instead, let's think of what we could put into the hands of Jesus for him to bless and use.*

*'A little in the hands of Jesus can become much.'*

**Prayer:** *Lord, grant me the heart of a cheerful giver.*

# Simon Peter
## On this rock

Day 17

*And so I tell you, Peter, you are a rock, and on this rock foundation I will build my church, and not even death will be able to overcome it.*

Matthew 16:18 Good News Bible

Simon Peter is the best known, most often mentioned and most charismatic of the apostles. When called by Jesus to follow him, he was a working fisherman, married, with his own home and family. By any account, he was a complex character: headstrong, impulsive, passionate, but sometimes failing to live up to his own expectations and those of others.

Yet from the beginning Peter was singled out by the Lord for special attention and instruction. Early on, Jesus declared that Peter was to be 'the rock', on which the new church of believers would stand (*Matthew 16:18*). As time went by, it might seem that he'd been mistaken in his choice. Peter is sometimes sharply rebuked by Jesus for his lack of faith and failure to properly respond to his teaching *(Matthew 14:31, Matthew 16:21-23, Mark 8:31-33, John 13:1-10)*. Peter sleeps while his Lord suffers in Gethsemane (*Mark 14:37*). He responds with violence when Jesus is seized (*John 18:10*). He deserts him in his hour of need and flees, and finally denies his relationship with him in a burst of oaths and cursing (*Mark 14:66-72*).

But the Lord knows Peter better than he knows himself, and he had not been mistaken in him. He sees beyond the human weakness and faults of temperament, to the heart of Peter, who loves him and passionately desires to serve and follow him.

After the resurrection, when the followers of Jesus are huddled together in grief and black despair, the Lord sends a special message, 'But go, tell my disciples, *and Peter,* "he is going ahead of you into Galilee. There you will see him, just as he told you"'

*(Mark 16:7).* He wants Peter to know that he is still included, still loved, that he is forgiven and will yet be 'the rock'.

What comfort to know that despite our worst mistakes and failures, there is still forgiveness and restoration, that God's plans for us still hold good. He does not abandon us when we fail, and look for someone better. Lovingly and tenderly he picks us up, dusts us off, puts us on our feet again and points us in the right direction.

**Reflection:** *Are there times when you feel you have failed the Lord so badly that he can have no possible further use for you? Is it difficult to accept his forgiveness? Or is it even more difficult to forgive yourself? Rejoice in the fact that our sins are washed away, that we are covered with the righteousness of Jesus.*

**Prayer:** *Lord, despite my many failures and weaknesses, my will is set to follow you.*

*Mould me and make me into what you would have me to be.*

# The Syro-Phoenician Woman
## Persistent asking

Day 18

*Ask and it will be given to you; seek and you will find; knock, and the door will be opened to you. For everyone who asks receives; he who seeks finds; and to him who knocks, the door will be opened.*

Matthew 7:7 NIV

**Reading:** Mark 7:24-30

This woman desperately wanted her daughter to be set free from the demons that held her. She came crying out to Jesus and pleading for his help, making such a nuisance of herself that the disciples became exasperated and asked him to send her away. After all, she had nothing to recommend her, not even being of the house of Israel – Greek by birth, Syro-Phoenician by nationality. But she recognised the Messiah and addressed him by name *(Matthew 15:22).*

Strangely, Jesus appears to completely ignore her. This seems totally out of character and unlike the compassionate healer he had proved himself to be.

Does this ring bells in our own experience? Are there times when we come to God in desperation, pleading help for deep needs, and have the feeling of butting our heads against a brick wall?

However, the woman did not go away, nor was she silenced. Yet when Jesus finally spoke to her, his answer seemed flatly discouraging. His mission was not to Gentiles such as she, he said. Nevertheless, she knelt at his feet and humbly repeated, one more time, her plea for help.

Again, his words were not encouraging. It would not be right, he said, to take the children's bread and give it to the dogs. Even then she did not give up. She said, 'Yes, Lord, but even the dogs eat the crumbs that fall from the master's table.'

And, suddenly, the light came on. Jesus commended her faith and gave her what she asked for.

Why did he seem reluctant, even hard and uncaring? Why did he not grant her request right away? Could it be that he was impressed from the start by her faith in him, and wanted to help her develop an even stronger faith? At every seeming rebuff, her determination grew. Against all the odds, she persisted, and was rewarded.

**Reflection:** *Do we ever feel that other people's prayers have more merit than our own, and are more likely to be answered? Or vice versa? Are we often tempted to give up if our prayers are not answered as promptly as we would like?Think about times in your own experience when persistence has been rewarded.*

**Prayer:** *Lord, teach us to pray, humbly but persistently.*

# The Demon-possessed Boy

## A father's faith

Day 19

*Faith comes by hearing, and hearing by the word of God.*

Romans 10:17 King James

**Reading:** Mark 9:14-29

This boy suffered from what we know today as epilepsy; he was also deaf and dumb. If you've ever seen a person having an epileptic fit, or a child with a febrile convulsion, you'll know how terrifying it is to witness. The boy's seizures seemed to be particularly violent, frequent and often life-threatening (*Mark 9:17-18).* The disciples had not been able to drive out the evil spirit.

Jesus seems exasperated with them, the way parents often are with children – 'how many more times do I have to tell you?' (*Mark 9:19).* Then he commands that the boy be brought to him and asks the father for a brief medical history. The father ends with the heartfelt plea, 'If you can, please help!'

Jesus replies 'If? There are no "ifs" among believers! Anything can happen!' *(Mark 9:23, The Message).*

The boy's father exclaims, 'I do believe! Help me with my doubts!'

And at the command of Jesus, the evil spirit comes out and the boy is restored to normality.

The question then arose as to why the disciples had failed to deliver the boy, and Jesus replies that this kind of demon only came out as a result of prayer. Some accounts mention fasting too. In Matthew's Gospel they are rebuked for their lack of faith *(Matthew 17:20-21).* It all seems to underline the fact that Jesus stayed in close contact with his Father at all times, spent much time in prayer, was filled with the Holy Spirit and ready at all times to do what was required of him.

The father of the boy demonstrated that he was going along the right lines. At first he was not sure whether Jesus had power enough to deal with the strong spirit that held his son. When given a little more instruction, he showed his willingness to grow in faith. And he knew that Jesus himself was the one who could supply that faith.

**Reflection:** *Think about faith, its nature and its source. Faith is a gift of God (Ephesians 2:8). Every one of us has a measure of faith (Romans 12:3). We only need the tiniest pinch to see miracles happen (Matthew 17:20). God gives faith, he grows it in us, and he is himself the one in whom our faith rests.*

**Prayer:** *Lord, I believe; help thou my unbelief (Mark 9:24).*

# The Woman Taken in Adultery

## A new and living way

Day 20

*See, I am doing a new thing! Now it springs up; do you not perceive it?*
Isaiah 43:19 NIV

**Reading:** John 8:3-11

How much the Pharisees and teachers were really bothered about the sinfulness of the woman is a debatable point. It seemed that the main object of their bringing her to Jesus was to catch him out and discredit his ministry. If his teaching continued to prevail, their own status and authority would be much diminished.

They were pretty sure they had Jesus in a cleft stick this time. If he said the woman should be stoned to death, as demanded by the law of Moses, he would be defying the Roman law, which did not allow the Jews to pass such sentences. If he said she should not, he denied the laws of Moses regarding adultery. Either way, he was in trouble, and they might have the means to get rid of him. Which way would he jump?

Jesus never turned a hair. Coolly and deliberately, he stooped and wrote words in the sand with his finger. Then, without any hurry, he invited the person who was without sin in the group to throw the first stone. And again he wrote on the ground.

No stones were thrown. Instead, one by one, the accusers sheepishly slipped away until only he and the woman were left. No one had been able to condemn her, and neither did Jesus. Instead, he offered her the gift of free forgiveness, and her life was transformed.

There's been speculation about the words Jesus wrote. I feel he may have been demonstrating the fact that a new way had been made, a new law written, not confined to the harsh and punitive Jewish and Roman laws, but the new law of God's grace and mercy he had come to proclaim, the free forgiveness that could be obtained by repentance and trust.

**Reflection:** *Can you remember times and situations when decisions had to be made and when all of the options seemed unthinkable? God has a way of providing new ways that no one has even dreamed of. He did it with Abraham and Isaac (Genesis 22). He did it at the Red Sea (Exodus 14). He's done it in the lives of myriad people who will trust him. He can do it for you and for me.*

**Prayer:** *Thank you, Lord, that in you old things are passed away, and all things are become new.*

# Mary of Bethany
## At the feet of Jesus

Day 21

*Mary has chosen what is better . . .* Luke 10:42 NIV

**Reading:** Luke 10:38-42

Like anyone else, Jesus needed friends as he travelled on his earthly journey. The house in Bethany, home of Mary, Martha and Lazarus, must have been a welcome haven for him to come to rest and relax. Jesus loved the three *(John 11:5)* and valued the friendship they offered.

From the outset, Mary seems to have been the one who 'latched on' to the true identity of Jesus as Saviour and Son of God. Time and again, she is found at his feet, worshipping him in adoration. She sits at his feet listening to his teaching and is rebuked by her sister for failing to help with the dinner (*Luke 10:39-40).* When Lazarus dies, she falls at his feet lamenting her loss and imploring his help *(John 11:32).* She passionately and extravagantly anoints his feet with precious ointment and dries them with her own hair *(John 12:3).* Her devotion does not go unnoticed. Jesus commends her attitude and will not hear a word against her.

Once she has met her Saviour, Mary cares little for the opinions of others. Her sister's scoldings, or even the outraged scorn of those professing to care about the poor, have no power to touch her. Her Lord has come, and she belongs to him heart and soul.

Many of us have this overwhelming love for the Lord when we first come to faith in him. We would go anywhere, do anything for him. As in a human love affair, this honeymoon period may not always last that long. Hopefully, it is replaced by a strong, loving commitment. But often the stresses and worries of life, its problems, concerns and cares, crowd in and come to the fore. The relationship with the Lord gets pushed back a little. We cool off a bit. The urgent things of life get in the way.

Jesus was first in Mary's life? Is he first in ours?

**Reflection:** *Any relationship needs commitment, time, communication, if it is to flourish. Think about our relationship with the Lord. His love for us is steadfast and unchanging. Have we lost our first love? Ask for the grace to love as Mary did.*

**Prayer:** *Lord, it is my chief complaint, that my love is weak and faint, yet I love, thee, and adore; O for grace to love thee more.*

W. Cowper, *Redemption Hymnal*

# Martha
## Learning and Growing

Day 22

> *. . . you are worried and upset about many things, but only one thing is needed.* Luke 10:41 NIV

**Reading:** Luke 10:38-41

Which of us who are 'chief cooks and bottle washers' in our homes have not sometimes felt a sneaking sympathy for Martha? I have! I want to be a 'Mary' and it's frustrating to be stuck in the kitchen over a hot stove while fascinating conversation with guests is going on elsewhere. Of course, a little forward planning can work wonders. A big casserole that cooks itself, food prepared earlier, even a takeaway, can ensure that nobody feels left out.

Maybe Martha could have planned things better, or simplified the meal. In any event, Jesus doesn't listen to her complaints about Mary's laziness. He knew that spending time with him was what both sisters needed most.

Martha seems to have taken his words to heart. Later, when their brother is desperately sick and then dies, it is she who goes to meet and greet him. She and Mary both need comfort, but Martha can't help having a grouse at Jesus for not coming in time to save her brother. Nevertheless, she has faith to believe that even now it is not too late *(John 11:22).*

There follows a remarkable conversation about eternal life in which Martha clearly demonstrates her growing faith and trust and is rewarded with the breathtaking revelation that Jesus himself is the resurrection and the life. And Martha is generous enough to want to include her sister Mary in the wonderful truths she is experiencing.

As her relationship with the Lord changes and deepens, Martha herself is changed. I am sure she still showed gracious hospitality, but hopefully no longer got so worried and upset about it.

**Reflection:** *Are we principally Marys or Marthas? The attributes of both are needful and valuable. Hospitality is needed and commended, but do we sometimes entertain more lavishly than necessary, because we enjoy the praise we get? Think about the words of Jesus: Mary has chosen the better part.*

**Prayer:** *Father, help me to serve without being unduly fussed or flustered, even if I'm left with the washing up! Help me to choose the 'better part' whenever I can – to sit at the feet of Jesus and learn from him.*

# Lazarus
## Back to life

Day 23

*. . . in him we live and move and have our being.* Acts 17:28 NIV

**Reading:** John 11:1-44

Not very much is known about Lazarus of Bethany, in fact not a word that he says is recorded in the Gospels. Yet he was a dearly loved young man, not only by his two sisters but also by Jesus, who had become a close friend.

Strange then that, on hearing that Lazarus was ill, Jesus didn't at once hurry to Bethany to deal with it. In fact, he deliberately delayed his going by several days, by which time Lazarus had already died. Yet, on meeting the grieving sisters and their friends, Jesus wept also.

Jesus knew that Lazarus would be miraculously brought back to life and that God would be glorified. Why, then, did he weep at the grave of Lazarus?

The answer of course lies in his dual nature. He was fully God, with authority over even life and death, but had also chosen to become fully man, with all the emotions and feelings that come with being human. He wept at the loss of a friend, and in empathy with the heartbroken sisters.

Jesus is not someone who cannot hear the heart cries of humanity or who does not understand pain, loss and sorrow. He knows when we hurt and he is close to the brokenhearted. He knows the shadowy places we walk through, the struggle, the conflict, the strife. He knows when our marriages break up, our children go astray, our businesses collapse and friends let us down. He understands the grief of losing a loved one. And he comes alongside, carries our heavy burdens and offers comfort and his transforming, lifegiving power.

Later, there was rejoicing and celebration at Bethany, when Jesus and Lazarus sat together at a special dinner party. By then, news had got round and both their lives were in danger. But despite trouble in store, their joy was complete.

**Reflection:** *Meditate on Isaiah 53:4 (King James): 'Surely he hath borne our griefs and carried our sorrows.' Two things stand out from these few words. (1) Grief and sorrow are heavy, crushing burdens to carry. (2) Jesus has already taken the weight himself, and willingly helps us carry it.*

**Prayer:** *Thank you, Lord, that you do not allow us to struggle alone under our heavy loads of grief and sorrow and sin. Help us to cast all our cares upon you, and know that you truly care for us.*

# The Children

## Greatest in the kingdom

Day 24

*He (Jesus) called a little child, and had him stand among them. And he said: 'I tell you the truth, unless you change and become like little children, you will never enter the kingdom of heaven.'*

Matthew 18:2-3 NIV

*(Jesus) said to them, 'Let the little children come to me, and do not hinder them, for the kingdom of God belongs to such as these. I tell you the truth, anyone who will not receive the kingdom of God like a little child will never enter it.' And he took the children in his arms, put his hands on them and blessed them.* Mark 10:14-16 NIV

At the time of Jesus, women and children did not enjoy the status that is taken for granted in our day and age. The welfare of children would depend on the family they were born into. Children could be sold as slaves, and the practice of 'exposing' unwanted babies – leaving them to die in the open – was used in Roman and Greek cultures.

When the disciples saw a group of women bringing their babies and children to Jesus to be blessed by him, they bristled with indignation. How dare these ignorant, chattering women bother the master and take up his time with something so trivial and unimportant?

As often happened, Jesus turned this attitude on its head. 'Don't stop them,' he said. 'Let them come to me.' And he picked up the little ones and blessed them.

Jesus made the astonishing statement that we must 'become like little children' before we can enter his kingdom. What exactly did he mean by this?

It begins by being born again, starting life afresh by putting our trust in him for our eternal future. Small children are trusting – they have to be. They have no power, no wisdom or life experience and have to trust older people for their every need. We too have to look to God to supply all we need for our spiritual life and growth.

Small children are innocent. Their little minds and personalities need to develop before they can make sense of life with all its implications. They need careful nurture and instruction if they're to realise their potential. The destroying of innocence and failure to protect the young is one of the most evil things we face today, and will surely result in God's judgement.

Small children are teachable – curious, eager to learn, excited by new discoveries, thrilled at new prospects. Those teaching children have enormous responsibility and enormous opportunities.

Small children live in the moment. They do not fret unduly about what happened yesterday, they don't waste time and energy worrying about what might happen tomorrow. They are content to leave important matters in the hands of someone bigger and wiser who knows more than they do.

Small children are amenable to discipline, if they're trained in the right way. They learn not to make the same mistake too many times.

Small children know how to laugh and play unselfconsciously, secure in the knowledge that someone they love is watching over them.

This may be an idealised picture of childhood and, sadly, there are too many children who can't experience it. But everyone, of whatever age, can 'become as a little child' and enter the kingdom of heaven, knowing God as the Father who waits with open arms to bless them.

**Reflection:** *Whether or not you have children in your life, imagine a world without children, and think of how dull, how depressing and how pointless it would be. Children today often seem to have so much materially, but miss out on things like family time, discipline and freedom. Think of ways you could make the world a better place for children to be.*

**Prayer:** *Father, grant me the simple faith and trust of a little child.*

# The Rich Young Ruler
## Too much to lose

Day 25

*. . . go, sell your possessions and give to the poor, and you will have treasure in heaven . . .* Matthew 19:21 NIV

**Reading:** Matthew 19:16-30

This young man really wanted to know what Jesus was about. He respected his status, fell on his knees before him and asked the question on his mind. When questioned himself, he revealed that he knew the laws well and had done his best to keep them.

Jesus looked at him and loved him *(Mark 10:21)*. Whether it was his honesty, his openness, or his sincere desire for the truth that particularly touched the heart of the Saviour, who can tell. The young man sounds like an attractive personality; he was wealthy, richly clothed and with many possessions. But Jesus knew something more was needed.

Jesus told him, 'Sell what you have, give to the poor and come follow me.'

The young man's face fell. He enjoyed his wealth and possessions. This was asking too much. Sadly, he went away.

Wealth can be a stumbling block for many of us. We have a tendency to want more and to hang on to what we already have. Wealth is not wrong in itself, but it does have power to change and to corrupt. We may tell ourselves we'd do lots of good if we had more money, but if we're honest, wouldn't it be tempting to spend at least some on ourselves, or save it for a rainy day? Wealth can bring with it a false feeling of independence, and that isn't always good in our relationship with God. No wonder Jesus made the remark about camels and the eyes of needles! *(Mark 10:25)*.

The poor were always very close to the heart of Jesus. As his followers, we have a clear commission to share what we have with those less fortunate. How we do this depends to some extent on our own circumstances and on the way God guides. We need to be open to that guidance.

**Reflection:** *Why do you think the young man could not have kept his wealth and followed Jesus too? Was Jesus testing him to see his reaction? Was the way still open for him to receive Jesus? Have we any regrets about money we have given to help those less fortunate?*

**Prayer:** *Take my silver and my gold; not a mite would I withhold;*
*take my intellect, and use every power as thou shalt choose.*

Frances Ridley Havergal, *Redemption Hymnal*

# The Pharisees
## Blind leaders of the blind

Day 26

*If the blind lead the blind, both shall fall into the ditch.*

Matthew 15:14 King James

The Pharisees (in Hebrew the title means the Separated Ones) were the largest of the three main religious parties in operation at the time of Christ. They were extremely powerful, influential and respected in the synagogue and in the community. The Pharisees rigorously upheld the Old Testament laws and were of high moral standing.

Into their midst came a young carpenter from Nazareth who threatened to turn their well-ordered life upside down. Suddenly, he was everywhere, travelling the countryside, preaching and teaching in the synagogue, healing the sick, doing miraculous deeds, attracting crowds in their thousands and claiming – horrors! – that he was the promised Messiah, the Son of God!

Shock waves went through the Pharisee community. This young upstart was turning their well-established beliefs on their heads. They expected a Messiah, but surely this man could not be he! Sadly, most of them (with a few exceptions) did not take the time to enquire further, to listen, and to study again their well-loved prophecies. Instead, they jumped on what they saw as his infractions of their laws, and allowed their eyes to be blinded to the truth. The threatened and worried Pharisees hardened their hearts and began to hatch plots to get rid of Jesus, one way or another.

It is tragic that the Pharisees reacted in this way. Jesus had come not to do away with their laws but to fulfil them *(Matthew 5:17-18).* Jesus had harsh words for the Pharisees, for their spiritual blindness, their hardness of heart, and for their unconcern for the deprived, needy and weak. They could have joined with him and become a great power for good; instead they chose to reject him and cling tight to their own closed, self-righteous, self-serving way of life.

**Reflection:** *What do you think Jesus meant by straining out a gnat and swallowing a camel? Are there modern equivalents in our present-day world governments and social leaderships? Why do some leaders and respected people seem blind to the truth of the gospel?*

**Prayer:** *Open our eyes, Lord, we want to see Jesus.*

Robert Cull, *© 1976 CCCM Music*

# The Ten Lepers
## A thankful heart

Day 27

*If the only prayer you say in your life is thank you, that would suffice.* Meister Eckhart (1260-1327/8)

*God has two dwellings, one in heaven and the other in a meek and thankful heart.* Isaak Walton (1593-1683)

**Reading:** Luke 17:11-19

These ten men from the border country had heard of Jesus and his power to heal and save. Pitiable and deformed, outcasts of society, they dared not come close to him, but stood at a distance and called out to him for help. Usually Jesus encouraged people to come near enough for him to touch them, but he didn't do that this time. His methods of healing were many and various, from a simple touch or a straight command, to plastering a mixture of mud and spit on the eyes of a blind man. He had no magic 'formula' or set routine.

But he expected obedience. This time, he simply told the men to show themselves to the priest, the customary procedure for anyone healed and cleansed of infectious disease. As they obeyed, the leprosy left them.

Nine of them just could not wait to rejoin society and get on with their lives. All the joys of normal life were now theirs again – they could kiss their children, embrace their wives, eat with friends, chat with neighbours, do their work – all things denied to them for so long.

Only one – the most unlikely of all, as he was a Samaritan from the wrong side of the border, despised by the Jews – took the time to go back to thank and praise the one who had performed his personal miracle. Jesus was saddened. All ten had obeyed him and been blessed, but only one had shown gratitude.

How often do we take for granted the blessings we enjoy? Are we truly thankful for health, work, freedom, families, friends, homes, holidays and so much more? And what about the precious gifts of clean water, air to breathe, green leaves, birdsong, mobility, laughter . . . the list is endless.

**Reflection:** *List twenty things we can thank God for, and then give thanks for each.*

**Prayer:** *Praise God from whom all blessings flow*
*praise him all creatures here below*
*praise him above, ye heavenly host*
*praise Father, Son and Holy Ghost.*

Thomas Ken (1637-1711), *Manual of Prayers 1674*

# James and John
## The upside-down kingdom

Day 28

*My kingdom is not of this world.* John 18:36 NIV

**Reading:** Mark 10:32-45

James and John were among the first disciples called by Jesus to follow and work with him. Along with another fisherman, Simon Peter, they shared in many special and significant occasions with the Lord. However, these young brothers were still on a steep learning curve, and did not always understand what they were being taught. On the last journey to Jerusalem, Jesus took the twelve aside and told them in plain terms the sequence of the arrest, trial, death and resurrection that lay ahead. The response of James and John was to approach Jesus and ask a special favour: that they would have the most important positions next to him when he came into his kingdom.

Matthew's Gospel has it that their mother made the request; maybe she was the typical pushy parent, wanting the best for her sons.

Jesus was patient with the pair of ambitious and eager young men, explaining why this could not be. The other disciples, however, had no hesitation in tongue-lashing the two for their ignorance and presumption. Again, Jesus calls them to order, and, as he often did, used the occasion for an object lesson in humility, reminding them that he himself had come not to be served, but to be a servant of all, and that the rules in his kingdom would be very different from the rules of the world.

Not for nothing has the rule of God been referred to as the upside-down kingdom. We read again and again of the powerful and mighty brought low, the weak and poor exalted, the least being first and the greatest last. The kingdom of God begins here and now, in the hearts of believers, but the time is also coming when justice and peace will reign in the earth, when 'every knee should bow . . . and every tongue confess that Jesus Christ is Lord' *(Philippians 2:10-11 NIV).*

**Reflection:** *In what ways would you like to see the kingdom of God at work in today's world? How can we work towards the coming of the kingdom? What do we feel about personal ambition? What, truthfully, are our own ambitions?*

**Prayer:** *That others may be loved more than I,*
*Jesus, grant me the grace to desire it.*

Rafael Cardinal Merry del Val (1865-1930)

# Blind Bartimaeus
## Sight restored

Day 29

*I want to see.* Mark 10:51 NIV

**Reading:** Mark 10:46-52

Jesus was on his last fateful journey to Jerusalem when he encountered the blind beggar by the roadside near Jericho. He appears to have been a familier figure along this route, known by name. He had heard of Jesus, too, and when he learns who it is approaching with the large crowd following, he immediately begins to call out in a loud voice.

This didn't go down too well, and he was told rather sharply to shut up. Maybe some found him an embarrassment. Are we sometimes embarrassed when unexpected people come into our well-ordered church services – the mentally unstable, the homeless, the giggling teenagers, or – horrors! – the noisy and talkative drunk? Do we discreetly usher them out or, at best, ask them to wait quietly in another room until someone can speak to them? Heaven forbid that our well-ordered service should ever be interrupted!

Jesus never minded an interruption, even if he was on his way to an urgent appointment or a sick friend. He always found time to speak to someone who needed him. His life was building to a huge climax, his earthly time was short and he knew it. But still he stopped and asked the man to come to him.

Contrast the reply of Bartimaeus with that of James and John, who had been asked the same question just hours before. 'What do you want me to do for you?' Young, ambitious and eager, they had wanted privilege and position. The request of Bartimaeus was simple: 'I want to see.'

And his faith was rewarded, his sight restored. Immediately Bartimaeus joined the crowd following Jesus, with everyone giving praise to God.

**Reflection:** *Why do you think Jesus never passed by anyone who came to him asking for help? What were the two immediate results of the meeting of Bartimaeus with Jesus? What would be an equivalent situation in our own society? What would be our reply if we were asked this question by Jesus?*

**Prayer:** *To hands that work, and eyes that see, give wisdom's heavenly lore,*
*that whole and sick, and weak and strong may praise thee evermore.*

E. H. Plumptre

# Zacchaeus
## A changed life

Day 30

*Today salvation has come to this house.* Luke 19:9 NIV

**Reading:** Luke 19:1-10

Zacchaeus was a man without many friends. The nature of his profession – tax collecting – made him an unpopular figure in Jericho, and he was dishonest with it, often extorting more money than taxes demanded to line his own pockets. No wonder he was disliked and despised.

Now he had heard some interesting gossip – that Jesus, the teacher from Galilee, was on his way to Jericho. And that he had healed a blind man that very morning. Zacchaeus made up his mind to see for himself this man with supernatural powers.

It was easy to tell when Jesus arrived in any village by the number of people surrounding him. Zacchaeus was a small man and couldn't even see the teacher in the milling mass of bodies. Nobody was going to let Zacchaeus have any privileges either, or usher him to the front to get a good view. So, spotting a sycamore tree some way ahead, he hurried down the road and climbed into its branches.

He had a good view from here and could see Jesus plainly, but to his astonishment Jesus noticed him too. Not only did the Saviour call him by name, but he told him to come down from the tree and prepare a place for him to stay that night.

Zacchaeus had got a little more than he bargained for, not just a sight of Jesus, but the huge privilege of giving hospitality to him. And having Jesus in his home and life brought dramatic changes. Not only did he offer half his possessions to the poor, but he determined to return four times the amount to everyone he had overcharged.

Zacchaeus was truly a changed man. He had gone out in the morning curious about the latest bit of gossip, and by nightfall had encountered the one with power to transform him.

**Reflection:** *Can you remember your first encounter with Jesus? Was it a life-changing experience? Think of some practical as well as spiritual ways in which your life has changed since you've known Jesus.*

**Prayer:** *Lord, make me willing to allow you into every part of my life, and to make me what I should be.*

# The Man with the Donkeys

## A part to play

Day 31

*See, your king comes to you, gentle and riding on a donkey, on a colt, the foal of a donkey.* Matthew 21:5 NIV

**Reading:** Matthew 21:1-11

There does not appear to have been any prior arrangement for the use of the donkeys at Bethphage, as far as their owner was concerned. Two of the disciples were despatched to pick them up. They were told that they would be questioned, and told the reply they must give. They even knew that the donkeys would be tied at a certain doorway in the village.

This event had been foretold by prophets many years before it came to pass. It had been planned by God to the tiniest detail, and none of it happened by chance. Always in close communion with his Father, Jesus knew and expected this sequence of events.

The owner of the donkeys was clearly taken aback when his animals were commandeered, out of the blue. Maybe he angrily chased them down the street as they were led away. But his attitude changed in a moment when he was given the simple message Jesus had sent: 'The Lord has need of them.'

This man may have been one of the disciples, or one of the thousands who had listened to the teachings of Jesus. In any event, he recognised the authority of the message, and the fact that he had a part to play in lending the donkeys for the last fateful journey to Jerusalem. He would have no idea of the unfolding drama that lay ahead, or how small or large a part his donkeys had to play, but he was obedient, and he took his place in God's plan.

**Reflection:** *Consider for a moment the breathtaking thought that our lives are planned, moment by moment, by the master hand of our Father*

*God. We have a choice about whether or not we'll fit into that plan. Even the smallest act of obedience can have far-reaching consequences. How can we be sure of hearing God's voice as we live our daily lives?*

**Prayer:** *Father God, thank you that we are all part of your 'big picture'. Help us to have ears to hear, and hearts that are willing and ready to obey.*

# The Teacher of the Law

## Leaving the comfort zone

Day 32

*Love the Lord your God with all your heart and with all your soul and with all your mind and with all your strength. The second (commandment) is this: Love your neighbour as yourself.*

Mark 12:30-31 NIV

**Reading:** Mark 12:28-34

This teacher appears to be genuinely curious to know more about the way Jesus is expounding the Scriptures. He notices his good answers to the questions of the Pharisees and Sadducees, despite the fact that many of them were 'trick' questions designed to catch him out.

And he approves of the opinion of Jesus as to the most important commandment. Jesus commends his wisdom and understanding, and tells him he is not far from the kingdom of God. The teacher seems to have grasped the message Jesus came to proclaim, the message of redeeming love. Many of the others were not willing to proceed beyond strict adherence to the letter of the law, a stumbling block that caused them to be stuck fast. This teacher saw that the mercy of God reached far beyond the customary sacrifices and burnt offerings. Perhaps he already had an inkling that the blood of Jesus would accomplish immeasurably more than all the shed blood of goats and bulls on their altars could ever do *(Hebrews 9:13-14)*.

Are we ourselves truly set free from the 'letter of the law'? Is there a danger that our church traditions and teachings can come to mean more than a living relationship with the Lord Jesus Christ? Do our busy programmes sometimes crowd out time with him? And how about loving our neighbours as ourselves? Are we prepared to leave the 'comfort zones' of our own church structures and programmes and get involved in reaching out to others in our community?

**Reflection:** *All of us enjoy the uplift and 'warm fuzzy feeling' we get from joining in a praise and worship session. We love meeting together, having fellowship, sharing our lives and encouraging one another. Are we prepared to forgo some of this to spend time with those of our neighbours who never come through the church doors?*

**Prayer:** *Lord, help us to remember the parable you told to explain who our neighbour is. And help us to break through barriers of shyness, reserve, racial, cultural or social differences, our own likes or dislikes. Help us to see others as you see them and to reach out in your name.*

# The Disciples
## Lessons in love

Day 33

*A new command I give you: Love one another.* John 13:34 NIV

**Reading:** John 13, 14, 15

These chapters record a poignant episode as the journey of Jesus with his disciples enters its last days. With time growing short, Jesus graciously and tenderly reveals more about his own nature and that of his Father God. At their last Passover, symbolically and lovingly, he washes the feet of the twelve *(John 13:1-17).*

He predicts his betrayal, to the consternation of his friends *(John 13:21-30).*

And he gives them the command that they must love one another as he has loved them *(John 13:34-35).*

The church I belonged to for over thirty years has a large blue and gold text over its pulpit, stating simply 'Love One Another'. Do we as Christians fulfil this commission? Not always, I fear. Most Christian fellowships and communities have their difficulties, bickerings, jealousies and rivalries. There are often differences of doctrine and denomination, undercurrents, tensions. There are clashes of temperament, and leaders, in particular, often seem to come under attack. All of this can lead to a subtle erosion of love.

Yet the love is there. When one meets a fellow Christian for the first time, there is an immediate link, the recognition of another family member. For we are family. With all of our human failings and differences, we belong together. The first disciples were a motley crew, argumentative, slow, apt to miss important points, sometimes self-seeking, but they had one thing in common – they loved Jesus and he was central in their lives. As they grew and matured, filled with his Spirit, they accomplished wonderful things. And the love between them was there for all to see.

**Reflection:** *Think of the nature of love (1 Corinthians 13) and of its importance in our witness to the world. Is love just a feeling? Or is it actively praying for and seeking the good of others? How do we deal with people we find it difficult to love?*

**Prayer:** *Lord, help me to forget myself for others, my brothers,*
*that in giving myself I may teach myself to love.*

Michel Quoist, *France*

# Judas
## Tragic choices

Day 34

*And he went out, and it was night.* John 13:30 NIV

**Reading:** Matthew 26:47-50; 27:1-10

I find it difficult to write about Judas. Traditionally, he is seen as the figure of evil, the betrayer who put Jesus on the cross, the one beyond the pale.

Yet questions come to mind. Judas was one of the first twelve disciples, hand-picked by Jesus, chosen by him to be taught, to live, travel and share with him, to be close to him for a period of years. He was given the responsible job of stewardship for the group.

Certainly, Judas had his weaknesses. He was covetous, self-righteous, resentful and greedy. But the other disciples too were far from perfect: James and John were over-ambitious and revengeful; Thomas full of doubts; Peter denied his Lord with oaths and curses. The others all had their share of faults and weaknesses, as do all of us who call ourselves Christians. It is so easy to excuse our faults by pointing a finger at someone we think is worse.

It is clear that Jesus knew from the start who would betray him *(Matthew 26:20-25)*. Judas had a necessary part to play in the overall scheme of things, which seems a hard thing for us to understand. But God's ways are not our ways and his thoughts not our thoughts *(Isaiah 55:8)*.

Jesus loved Judas, as he loved all his disciples. Despite his failings, Judas comes over as a pretty ordinary man until the time of the Last Supper, when 'Satan entered into him' *(John 13:27)*. From then on he seems to be motivated by evil, malice and greed, which, when these had produced their results, turned to bitter remorse and despair. He had made the wrong choices, and regretted it too late.

On the cross, Jesus cried out, 'Father forgive them, for they know not what they do!' *(Luke 23:34)*. On whose behalf was this request made? Was it for the turncoat crowd who had cried out for his blood, for the Romans, the Jews, those who had misunderstood and denied and deserted him? Was it for all the sinners who would come after, for you and for me?

Was it for Judas too?

**Reflection:** *How do we truly feel about the mercy and forgiveness of God being extended to those who have committed terrible atrocities? Do we feel that there are some things which cannot be forgiven? Which do you think is greater, the sinfulness of the human heart or the grace and mercy purchased by Jesus on the cross?*

**Prayer:** *Lord, have mercy upon me, a sinner.*

# Caiaphas
## Unwitting prophet

Day 35

*You do not realise that it is better for you that one man die for the people rather than that the whole nation perish.* John 11:50 NIV

**Reading:** Matthew 26:57-67

Caiaphas, the Jewish High Priest at the time of the arrest and trial of Jesus, appears to have been a man of wealth, power and influence. He also officiated at the High Court to which Jesus was brought and accused of blasphemy.

Caiaphas and other influential Jewish leaders had been increasingly threatened and worried by the growing popularity of the teachings of Jesus, fearing both for their own positions and for their standing before the Romans. Plots had been hatched to kill him and, this time, they weren't about to let him slip through their fingers.

The trial of Jesus was a brutal travesty of justice, with false and conflicting evidence, and fury at the replies given by Jesus to his accusers. In their rage they allowed the guards to spit on him and play cruel games, blindfolding him and asking him to 'prophecy' by saying who had struck him. Later he was beaten up before being passed on to the Roman governer Pontius Pilate for sentencing.

Caiaphas proved himself to be cowardly, brutal and corrupt, but, strangely, he himself had spoken prophetic words about the one he persecuted *(John 11:49-50).*

Even Caiaphas unwittingly testified to God's purposes made manifest in his Son Jesus Christ, and played his part in the story of redemption.

**Reflection:** *Is it only the 'good guys' who have a part in God's plan? There are times when actions and words meant for evil have been turned*

*around by God to bring about good. Can you think of any such times in your own experience?*

**Prayer:** *Let the words of my mouth, and the meditation of my heart, be acceptable in thy sight, O Lord, my strength, and my redeemer.*

Psalm 19:14 King James

# Pontius Pilate
## What is truth?

Day 36

*Thy word is true from the beginning.* Psalm 119:160 King James

*You shall know the truth, and the truth shall make you free.*

John 8:32 King James

**Reading:** John 18:28-40

Pontius Pilate, as Governor of Judea, had the final say in the sentencing of Jesus after his 'trial'. From the outset, he seems to be reluctant to proclaim the death sentence, emphasising several times the fact that he can find no fault in Jesus. Was this partly due to the disturbing dream his wife had experienced, causing her to interrupt him in the very seat of judgement? *(Matthew 27:19).* Historical accounts record that she herself later became a believer.

It does seem that Pilate tried his hardest to shift the decision-making onto the crowd *(Matthew 27:24)* and made a show of public handwashing to absolve himself from any responsibility for the death sentence. Pilate is portrayed by some as being weak and vacillating, by others as corrupt and self-seeking, wanting to keep the favour of both the Jews and his Roman masters. It may be that his wife's dream had disturbed him more than perhaps seemed apparent, and that the demeanour and replies of Jesus disturbed him even more. Pilate asked 'What is truth?' when Jesus declared that everyone on the side of truth would listen to him *(John 18:38).*

But it appears that his own conscience already knew the answer and that Pilate chose to ignore the truth and take the easy and self-serving way *(John 18:39-40).*

History has it that the life of Pilate eventually ended in suicide. Was he, like Judas, filled with remorse for what he had done?

**Reflection:** *Think about the nature of truth. Is it always easy to follow one's conscience? Think about the many ways truth can be ignored, tweaked or 'bent' – by exaggeration, selective memory, suppressing unpleasant facts, gossip, bias or wishful thinking. Can we be absolutely certain that we are always truthful? Do we always tell the truth even when it will show us in a bad light?*

**Prayer:** *Lord, help us to speak the truth, and to speak it in love.*

# Simon of Cyrene

## Carrying the cross

Day 37

*As they were going out, they met a man from Cyrene, named Simon, and they forced him to carry the cross.* Matthew 27:32 NIV

**Reading:** Matthew 27:27–55

So here is Jesus, mocked, buffeted, beaten, scourged, and having his death sentence endorsed by a howling mob who only days before had shouted their hosannas as he rode into their city. Under Jewish law, he would have been stoned to death, but the leaders, wishing to be politically correct, decreed that he be executed according to Roman custom. So Jesus sets out on his last walk, carrying his cross to the place of execution.

The cross weighed heavily on him. Jesus was not a weak man; his shoulders would have been muscular and strong, used to manual labour. But the scourging and beating had taken their toll, his flesh was raw and bleeding, he was thirsty and exhausted. He stumbled. To hurry things along, the soldiers looked about for someone to help and spied a sturdy-looking countryman, Simon, just up from Cyrene. They didn't have to bother asking him for help. Anyone they chose was compelled by Roman law to carry goods for a mile. A prod from a Roman spear was all the request that was needed. Simon hadn't expected to be press-ganged into this job; he didn't volunteer, but nevertheless he hoisted the cross onto his broad shoulders and carried it to Golgotha.

For some years a group of Christians would carry a cross around our busy town each Good Friday. My husband made the cross; it was nothing fancy, just two solid beams of oak fastened together with a metal bolt. It was rough, hard and heavy, and took a strong man to carry it. We followers were a motley crew – students, middle-aged people, visitors, children, some elderly having to be helped along. I remember pushchairs and someone wheeling a bike. Sometimes people would join us, more often folk were indifferent, embarrassed, curious or amused. To those of us following, it was a precious thing to be identified with the cross, an uplifting yet humbling experience.

The cross of Jesus has become a symbol of Christianity, but it is still also a living reality today. Just yesterday I received an email from a friend, a young girl still in her twenties who has chosen to live and work in a war zone, where she is in constant danger from bombs, suicide attacks and kidnapping. She wrote of how in amazing ways the cross of Christ has enabled her to experience his heart for the people she lives among and his peace that passes all understanding, and how it has come to mean life and hope in a place shattered by death, hatred and despair.

Little is recorded of Simon after that fateful experience, though in later years his sons Rufus and Alexander were well-known members of the church in Rome. There is evidence to suggest that Good Friday was a life-changing day for Simon too.

**Reflection:** *Meditate for a while on the cross and on what it means in your own life.*

*Remember that Jesus had power to avoid the cross, but that he, the sinless one, chose to die in this way so that we could be freed for ever from sin and death. Ask God to give us a greater understanding of his sacrifice.*

**Prayer:** *Oh, make me understand it,*
*help me to take it in;*
*what it meant to thee, the Holy One,*
*to bear away my sin.*

Katherine A. M. Kelly, *Redemption Hymnal, © Copyright Control*

# The Dying Thief

Day 38

*Jesus, remember me when you come into your kingdom.*

Luke 23:42 NIV

**Reading:** Luke 23:32-43

Much has been written about the dying thief. He has been used as an illustration of the validity of 'deathbed conversions' – though there are those who insist he could not have been saved because he hadn't formally repented of his sins, he hadn't been baptised or proved his faith by works of restitution.

Nevertheless, the words of Jesus remain: 'I tell you the truth, today you will be with me in paradise' *(Luke 23:43)*. It appears that earlier in the day the thief had joined with the other one crucified with Jesus, in reviling and pouring scorn upon him *(Mark 15:32)*. Later, his attitude changes. At some stage during their terrible ordeal, he had come to believe that Jesus was no common criminal but that he was who he claimed to be, the Son of God. What changed his mind is not clear, but it seems likely that he had been convinced by the words of the one crucified next to him, by his demeanor and his attitude to those around him. No ordinary man could continue to love, forgive and care for others in the grip of such suffering.

In happier times, Jesus had illustrated God's heart for wandering sinners by telling the parable of the Prodigal Son. The son had demanded his inheritance (thus implying he wished his father dead), squandered it, been reduced to nothing and obliged to creep home in shame. The father never ceased loving him or looking out for his return. When he was just a tiny dot in the distance, the father ran to meet him with open arms – before he knew if the son was sorry, before he heard any details, before any apologies could be made. His son had come back to him, that was all that mattered.

So it was with the dying thief. As Moses lifted up the serpent in the wilderness, so that all might 'look and live', so the thief needed only to turn to the one lifted up on the cross beside him and acknowledge him as Lord and Saviour.

**Reflection:** *Let's remember that there are no degrees of sin, that all of us need to come to the Lord Jesus Christ and trust him for forgiveness and salvation.*

**Prayer:** *Jesus, thou art the sinner's friend,*
*as such I look to thee;*
*now, in the fullness of thy love,*
*O Lord, remember me.*

Richard Burnham

# John
## Loving and caring

Day 39

*I have loved you with an everlasting love; I have drawn you with lovingkindness.* Jeremiah 31:3 NIV

*Many waters cannot quench love; rivers cannot wash it away.* Song of Songs 8:7 NIV

**Reading:** John 19:25-27

In his Gospel, John never refers to himself by name, simply as 'the disciple whom Jesus loved'. Some opinions put this down to modesty, others that John was singled out in some way. Could it not have been simply that John was secure in the knowledge of how deeply and completely he was loved by Jesus? How many doubts, heart-searchings, and mistakes might be avoided if we could all rest continually in that knowledge.

John had not always been the perfect disciple. History has it that he was maybe only seventeen years old when he first met Jesus. Jesus himself called him a 'son of thunder'. John was very keen to be in a prominent position in God's kingdom (*Mark 10:35-41)*, and more than willing to call down fire on the heads of his enemies *(Luke 9:52-54)*.

Later, he was described as 'ignorant and unlearned' *(Acts 4:13)*. Yet later in life he wrote the most wonderful Gospel with its message of love, as well as the account of magnificent cosmic events in time and space in the book of Revelation.

In Gethsemane, with the other disciples, John had failed to keep watch and then had fled from those coming to arrest Jesus. But he is there at the cross, waiting and watching, with those close to the Lord. And Jesus knows the loving heart of John, and gives him a special commission: he is to take his own place as a son to Mary, and take care of her while she lives.

So the day wears on, with the Saviour carrying the weight of the world's sin as his life ebbs away. And then it is over. At his passing, it is as though creation itself cries out both in protest and in triumph; the sun is blotted out, the earth erupts and men long dead walk free from their tombs. Death has been conquered. The temple veil tears in two from top to bottom, and all humankind has a way to enter the presence of God. It is finished.

The sorrow as sharp as a sword, promised to Mary by Simeon when Jesus was an infant, has pierced her heart. But he has provided a human comforter for her in John.

**Reflection:** *Think about how John might have felt as he watched the one he loved so much suffer and die. Imagine how precious the last command of Jesus must have been to him, how carefully he would carry it out. During his ministry, there were times when Jesus spoke in what might seem a harsh way to both his disciples and to his mother. What does this last request show about the feelings that he had for them all?*

**Prayer:** *My Jesus, I love thee, I know thou art mine,*
*for thee all the pleasures of sin I resign;*
*my gracious Redeemer, my Saviour art thou,*
*if ever I loved thee, my Jesus, 'tis now.*

W. R. Featherston (1842-70), *Redemption Hymnal*

# Mary Magdalene
## Joy in the morning

Day 40

*I am he that liveth, and was dead; and, behold, I am alive for evermore.* Revelation 1:18 King James

*I am the resurrection, and the life: he that believeth in me, though he were dead, yet shall he live. And whosoever liveth and believeth in me shall never die.* John 11:25 King James

**Reading:** John 20:1-18

The day following the crucifixion was a black one indeed for the followers of Jesus. Not yet realising fully the truth of the resurrection, their hopes lay in ruins. Their Lord was dead. All that they could do for him now was grant him a decent burial, so the women went to work preparing embalming spices with which to anoint the body.

Among the women were Mary the mother of Jesus and Mary Magdalene. With others they had travelled with Jesus on his journeys, taking care of his day-to-day needs. They had followed him to the cross and stood beside him through the long day of his dying, and had clung together as they shed tears of bitter grief.

According to some historians, Mary Magdalene and Mary of Bethany were one and the same. It is commonly believed that Mary Magdalene was a prostitute – though in fact no mention of this is found in any of the Gospels. She had been delivered by Jesus of 'seven devils' – though this could also have applied to many that he encountered. Whatever the facts, it seems certain that Mary Magdalene had found forgiveness and new life in Jesus, that she loved her Lord and had served him faithfully.

Now, heartbroken, on the morning of the third day, she stands weeping outside the tomb. The body she had come to tend is gone. In despair, she piteously asks the man standing outside to tell her where it has been taken.

At first she does not recognise his voice. Maybe her grief is so overwhelming that her senses are dulled. It is only when he tenderly speaks her name – 'Mary!' – that the glorious truth bursts upon her. It is he! The half-understood event he promised has come to pass. He was dead, but is alive again!

He is risen! And suddenly the darkness is gone and new life and joy flood into her soul.

**Reflection:** *Think of the words of St Augustine: 'We are an Easter people, and Alleluia is our song!' And sing it! 'Alleluia! Alleluia! Alleluia!'*

**Prayer:** *You turned my wailing into dancing; you removed my sackcloth and clothed me with joy, that my heart may sing to you and not be silent.*

*O Lord my God, I will give you thanks for ever.* Psalm 30:11-12 NIV